THE MICROWAVE WAY

by Dorothy McNett

Illustrated by Martin Jacobs and Nita Ybarra

OWLSWOOD PRODUCTIONS COOKBOOKS
BUNDT CAKES by Karen Plageman and Susan Herbert
THE WOK WAY by Winnie Tuan
SLOW-CROCK COOKERY by Karen Plageman
THE CRÊPE BOOK by Susan H. Herbert
BAKE BREAD by Marguerite Bencivenga and Barbara Brauer
BRAVO! ITALIAN COOKING by Cynthia Scheer
FRENCH COUNTRY FAVORITES by Cynthia Scheer
NATURAL FIBER COOKING by Karen Plageman
GERMAN HOME COOKING by Cynthia Scheer
MEXICAN COOKING by Cynthia Scheer
THE FOOD PROCESSOR BOOK by Pam Biele and Susan Walter
THE MICROWAVE WAY by Dorothy McNett

TABLE OF CONTENTS

ABOUT THE AUTHOR

Dorothy McNett is a trendsetter. Her store in Sunnyvale, McNett's Microwave, was the first microwave specialty store in the San Francisco Bay Area. Its rapid success led to the opening of a second store in Redwood City. Now with both businesses thriving, Ms. McNett is a leading proponent of the microwave way to cook.

After graduating from the University of Northern Iowa, Ms. McNett was employed as a consultant by Magic Chef, a leading microwave oven manufacturer. Her enthusiasm about microwave cooking soon led Ms. McNett to teach classes in her home. In a short time, the demand for classes exceeded the confines of her kitchen and Ms. McNett realized the growing popularity of microwave cooking. It was then that she opened her first store.

Because she feels that knowing how to use the microwave oven is just as important as owning one, Ms. McNett offers microwave classes at her stores in addition to selling the ovens and accessories.

This is her first cookbook and consists of a sampling of her favorite recipes plus her tips on microwave cooking.

Introduction

Welcome to the world of microwave cooking! You can cook foods in just minutes with this remarkable space-age appliance. But more than that, foods cooked in a microwave oven retain their natural flavors, textures and colors. Vegetables cook to a tender crispness. Meats stay juicy. Sauces take only minutes and cook to a smooth perfection. And when you reheat leftovers, they taste as fresh as the first time around.

Today there are many microwave ovens on the market. They range from very basic ones on up to elaborate electronic wonders with many features. Even though the kinds of control settings available vary according to manufacturer and price, this cookbook is designed to be used with *all* microwave models.

Throughout this cookbook the terms FULL POWER, 3/4 POWER and HALF POWER are used. But with one look at your microwave oven, you can easily translate these terms to your own oven's controls. If your oven does not have variable control, alternative cooking times are always given in the recipes when necessary.

ELECTRONIC CONTROL

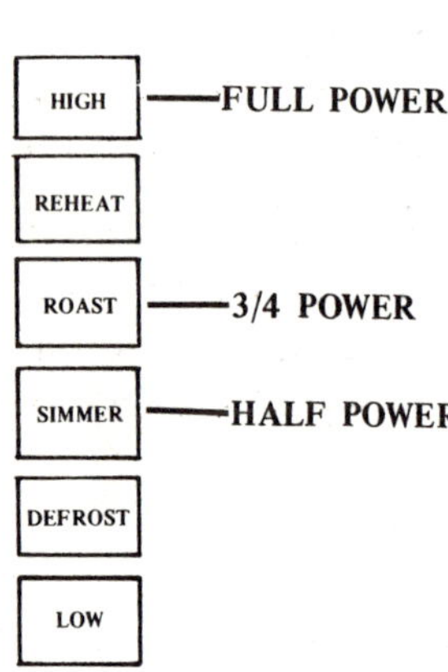

MANUAL CONTROL

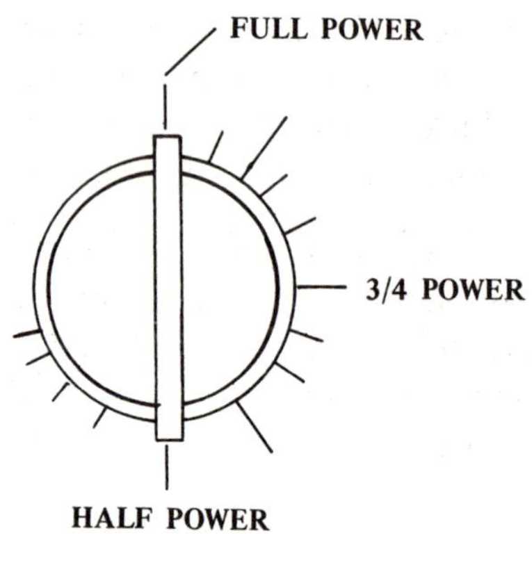

How does a microwave oven cook?

At the heart of every microwave oven is a tube called a magnetron. This magnetron tube generates the microwaves, a form of radiowave, and transmits them through a metal wave guide into the oven's interior. Microwaves cannot pass through metal, so they are contained by the metal interior of the oven.

Microwaves thus restricted to the interior of the oven are absorbed by the food. Foods containing moisture (water molecules) will cook because microwaves agitate the water molecules, creating friction that produces heat. (A paper towel in a microwave oven stays cool, because the towel is dry. So is the air in the oven, which also remains fairly cool.)

In cooking, this microwave energy penetrates about 1 to 2 inches into food from the outside surfaces, working its way into the center by thermal conduction. A thin piece of food, such as a 1-inch-thick sandwich, receives microwaves from all directions and warms up rapidly throughout. When cooking foods of this general shape, use FULL POWER and a short cooking time.

By contrast, a large piece of food, such as a roast, receiving microwave energy only in the outer 1 to 2 inches, needs a different treatment. The core of the roast remains cool until heat from the outside is conducted to the center. In this situation, use a lower power setting, if your microwave oven has one, and a longer cooking time. This assures more even cooking and avoids overcooking of the outside edges.

Get to know your microwave oven
Get acquainted with the way *your* microwave oven works. To get an idea of its speed, put 1 cup (8 oz.) tap water into the oven. Microwave it, *uncovered,* at FULL POWER, until the water boils. It should take from 2 to 4 minutes. If the time is closer to 2 minutes, use the shorter cooking times given in this book; if the time is closer to 4 minutes, use the longer cooking times.

Observe the hot spots in your microwave oven; they remain in the same places. In most late model microwave ovens, food needs little turning, as technology has improved the distribution of micro-wave energy. You can, however, open the oven door at any time to rotate the dish a quarter or half turn if the food seems to be cooking unevenly. In some microwave ovens a rotating shelf turns the food constantly, producing very even cooking.

Stirring also helps to distribute heat. Stir once, about halfway through the cooking time, and again when the food is done.

Choosing cookware for microwave cooking
Because microwaves cannot pass through metal, no metal cooking vessels can be used in a microwave oven. Instead, choose ceramic, glass or microwave plastics. Although cooking vessels don't absorb microwave energy, the food within them gets very hot, so some care must be used in selection.

You can use any heat-tempered glass, such as Pyrex or Anchor Hocking. Pottery can also be used, but it must not have a shiny metallic glaze that gets hot during cooking. Ovenware porcelain is a good choice, for it makes cooking and serving simple and elegant. Paper plates and paper towels are fine for reheating foods, but should not be used for extended cooking.

A simple test for suitability of a cooking vessel is to place it, empty, in the microwave oven at FULL POWER 20 to 30 seconds. If it stays cool, it is fine to use it. If the dish becomes warm or hot in this time, however, do not use it for microwave cooking.

Avoid containers with any metal trim. Microwave energy may cause this trim to spark or arc, damaging the trim and possibly the magnetron.

Casserole lids make good covers for your cooking containers. You can also use paper towels, waxed paper or plastic wrap. (Slit plastic wrap in the center to allow steam to escape.)

How to use your microwave oven for defrosting
Defrost meats—roasts, chicken, turkey and ground meat—in their paper or plastic freezer wrappings. If frozen foods are wrapped in foil, unwrap them, transfer the food to a plate or microwave roasting rack and cover loosely with waxed paper. In general, most meat products take 5 minutes per pound to defrost. Fish and seafood, which are more delicate, take 3 minutes per pound.

After defrosting, allow a standing period of the same amount of time to assure even thawing to the center. For example, microwave 1 pound of frozen ground beef at DEFROST 5 minutes, then let it stand 5 minutes. Now it is ready to cook. (For safety, always plan to cook defrosted foods within a few hours, as some surface heat will be created during defrosting.)

How to determine microwave cooking times

Microwave cooking times are determined by the *volume* of food to be heated or cooked. For example, 1 slice of bacon cooks in 1 minute and 3 slices take 3 minutes. This is because the amount of microwave energy is constant, and when it is absorbed by 3 pieces of food, each will get only 1/3 as much.

To calculate cooking times, multiply the time for 1 item, such as a potato, by the number to be cooked, then subtract 1/4 of that total. In the example of the potato, 1 cooks in 4 minutes:

$$4 \text{ potatoes} \times 4 \text{ minutes} = 16 \text{ minutes}$$
$$16 \text{ minutes} \div 4 \text{ minutes} = 4 \text{ minutes}$$
$$16 \text{ minutes} - 4 \text{ minutes} = 12 \text{ minutes approximate cooking time}$$

Check the potatoes at 12 minutes. If they aren't quite done, add on additional minutes as needed.

To determine the time to heat cooked food, use this general rule: 2 minutes per cup of food. For example, 3 cups of cooked macaroni and cheese (taken directly from the refrigerator) will take 6 minutes at most to heat in a microwave oven. Check it after 4 minutes by stirring, then by placing your hand on the bottom of the container. If it is too hot to hold your hand there comfortably, the food is ready to serve; if your hand feels only a little warmth, return the macaroni to the microwave oven for 2 minutes more.

Microwave cookware and accessories

Most new microwave cooks find they already have glass and pottery cookware that can be used in a microwave oven. There are, however, a few special microwave accessories that are useful to have.

• The plastic roasting rack takes the place of a conventional wire roasting rack. It is a must for roasts and can be used for cooking bacon and sausages and for heating baked goods. There are also specially designed plastic bacon racks available.

• Plastic baking dishes, including bundt cake forms, layer cake bakers, muffin or cupcake forms, cookie sheets and more.

• Meat thermometers, called "bi-therm" thermometers, contain no mercury and have either glass or plastic faces. These thermometers are extremely accurate and provide a temperature reading within 10 seconds. They must *never touch the oven's walls*. (If you plan to use the bi-therm thermometer in a conventional oven or with the broiling element in some microwave ovens, select a glass-faced one.)

• Browning dishes and grills are available in several sizes and shapes. The grills have a well around the edge to allow fat to drain during the cooking of steaks, chops or meat patties. The dishes have lids and can be used as casseroles. They are convenient for browning or sautéing before adding other ingredients. Check the manufacturer's instructions for preheating times.

• Glass measuring cups and "batter bowls" are available in several sizes. The 2-cup size is useful for sauces and gravies; the 4-cup and 8-cup batter bowls are handy for vegetables and puddings.

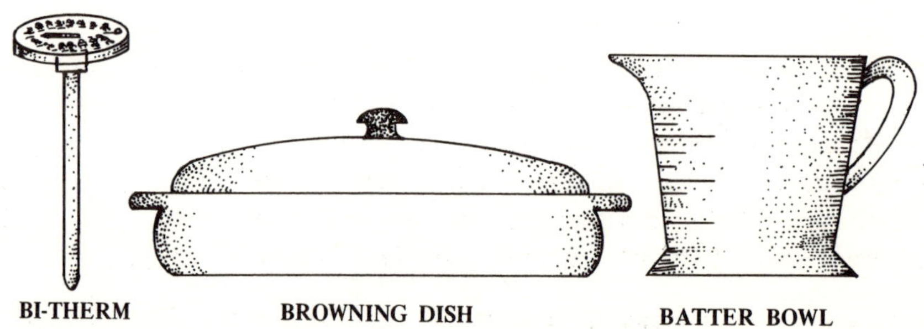

FIFTEEN-MINUTE POTATO SOUP
so quick and easy, this will become a favorite standby

4 medium potatoes, peeled and quartered
1/2 medium onion, finely chopped
3 to 4 cups milk
Salt and white pepper
Crumbled crisp bacon or toasted croutons, for garnish

Place potatoes and onion in large casserole. Microwave, *covered,* at FULL POWER 9 to 11 minutes, until potatoes pierce easily when tested with a fork. Mash with a potato masher, purée in a blender or food processor or put mixture through a food mill. Return to casserole, if necessary. Gradually mix in milk until smoothly blended, adding just enough to make desired consistency. Microwave, *uncovered,* at FULL POWER 4 to 5 minutes, until steaming hot but not boiling. Season to taste with salt and pepper. Serve sprinkled with bacon or croutons. Makes 6 servings.

Note: To use this soup as a basis for a seafood chowder, stir in cooked fish or shellfish before reheating with milk.

FRESH MUSHROOM SOUP
creamy and rich, with a hint of lemon

6 tablespoons butter or margarine
3 tablespoons flour
2-1/2 cups regular-strength chicken broth
1-1/4 cups milk
1/2 pound mushrooms, pressed through a coarse
   sieve or minced in food processor
3 tablespoons chopped parsley
Juice of 1 lemon
2/3 cup whipping cream
Salt and freshly ground pepper
1/4 cup whipping cream, whipped, for garnish
Toasted slivered almonds, for garnish (see note)

Place butter in a 2- to 3-quart casserole. Microwave, *uncovered*, at **FULL POWER** 30 to 45 seconds. Smoothly mix in flour. Gradually mix in chicken broth, then stir in milk, mushrooms, parsley and lemon juice. Microwave, *uncovered*, at **FULL POWER** 7 to 8 minutes. Mix in cream; heat 1 to 2 minutes. Taste and season with salt and pepper. Serve with a dollop of whipped cream and a sprinkling of almonds. Makes 4 servings.

Note: To toast the almonds, place 1/2 cup slivered almonds and 1 teaspoon butter in a small dish or measuring cup. Microwave, *uncovered*, at **FULL POWER** 2 to 3 minutes.

GOULASH SOUP

hot biscuits or French bread are good with this hearty main dish soup

1 large onion, chopped
1 green pepper, seeded and chopped
2 tablespoons salad oil
1 can (6 oz.) tomato paste
1 teaspoon salt
1/4 teaspoon freshly ground pepper
1 pound boneless top round steak, cut into
    1/2-inch cubes
6 cups hot water
Juice of 1 lemon
2 cloves garlic, minced or pressed
1 teaspoon caraway seed
2 tablespoons paprika (preferably sweet
    Hungarian paprika)

Combine onion, green pepper and oil in 4-quart casserole. Microwave, *uncovered,* at FULL POWER 4 minutes. Stir in remaining ingredients. Return to microwave oven, *covered,* at FULL POWER 10 minutes. Then reduce to HALF POWER and microwave 60 minutes longer, until meat is tender. (If your microwave oven does not have variable power, microwave at FULL POWER 40 to 50 minutes in all.) Taste and add salt, if needed. Makes 6 servings.

MINESTRONE WITH BEEF
serve this classic Italian soup with crusty French bread—it's a full meal!

1 pound beef stew meat, cut into 3/4- to 1-inch cubes
2 medium potatoes, peeled and cut into 1/4-inch cubes
2 medium zucchini, sliced 1/4 inch thick
2 medium carrots, sliced 1/4 inch thick
1 large onion, chopped
1 can (15 or 16 oz.) red kidney beans, drained
1 can (1 lb.) stewed tomatoes or whole tomatoes,
    broken up with a fork
2 cups tomato juice
1/2 cup broken spaghetti (1-inch pieces)
1 clove garlic, minced or pressed
1 head cabbage, shredded
4-1/2 cups water
1 bay leaf
1/2 teaspoon freshly ground pepper
2 teaspoons salt
Pinch crumbled oregano

In a large casserole, at least 4-quart size, combine all ingredients. Microwave, *covered*, at FULL POWER 20 minutes. Then microwave at HALF POWER 60 to 70 minutes, until meat is tender. (If your microwave oven does not have variable power, microwave at FULL POWER 40 to 50 minutes in all.) Taste and add salt, if needed. Makes 6 to 8 servings.

SAUCY SHRIMP

not really a soup — but so saucy you can serve it as a first course

2 pounds medium to large shrimp or prawns, shelled and deveined
1/2 cup *each* olive oil and dry white wine
1/4 cup lemon juice
3 cloves garlic, minced or pressed
1 teaspoon crumbled oregano
3 tablespoons chopped parsley
Salt and pepper
French bread

In a large casserole or shallow baking dish lightly mix all ingredients except salt, pepper and bread. Microwave, *covered*, at FULL POWER 4 to 5 minutes, stirring once. Season with salt and pepper to taste. Serve immediately with French bread to dunk into the sauce. Makes 24 appetizer servings, or 4 main-dish servings.

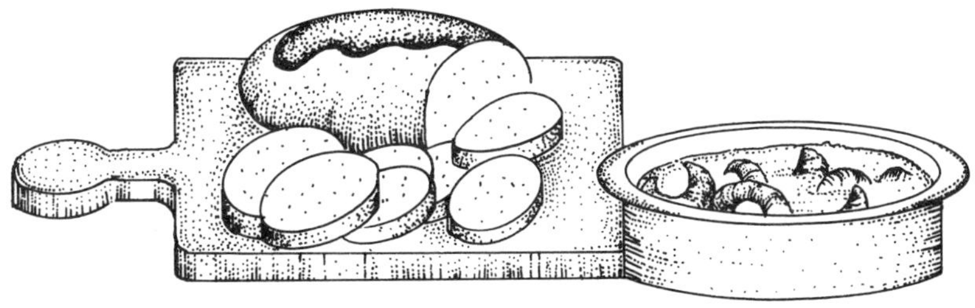

Meats, Poultry and Fish Dishes

STEAK WITH FRESH MUSHROOMS
a quick and delicious dinner for one or two

1/2 pound mushrooms, sliced
1 tablespoon butter or margarine
Porterhouse, T-bone or rib steak, 3/4 to 1 inch thick
Salt and pepper

Place mushrooms and butter in 1-quart casserole. Microwave, *covered*, at FULL POWER 2 to 3 minutes, or until mushrooms are tender. Set aside.

Preheat microwave browning grill (see page 12) in microwave oven at FULL POWER 4 minutes for small grill and 8 minutes for larger grill. Cut away extra fat around edge of steak; slit into fatty edge at about 1-inch intervals to prevent curling during cooking. *Do not salt before cooking,* as salt tends to dehydrate the meat.

Place steak on preheated grill. Microwave, *uncovered*, at FULL POWER 1 to 2 minutes. Turn to brown second side. Microwave 1 to 2 minutes more, to desired doneness. Season with salt and pepper to taste. Spoon mushroom sauce over steak. Makes 1 to 2 servings.

CHUCK ROAST WITH VEGETABLES
if your microwave oven has a variable control, try this delicious dish

The ideal roast for this dish is a 7-bone chuck roast (it gets its name from the most prominent bone, which resembles a figure 7). Other cuts that are suitable include round bone or pin bone chuck roasts.

Look for a roast with a minimum of bone and fat. Irregularly shaped roasts are not very satisfactory because the small, narrow end overcooks.

Cooking time will be 20 to 25 minutes per pound (200° internal temperature on a microwave meat thermometer or probe). The roast forms its own flavorful liquid as it cooks, although no liquid is added. When done, the meat will be tender-firm and will taste delicious.

To prepare the roast, sprinkle lightly on all sides with pepper and salt or seasoned salt. Place meat in a large covered casserole, about 4-quart size. Microwave, covered, at HALF POWER for half of the estimated cooking time. Turn, cover again, and continue cooking, adding vegetables during the last 20 to 25 minutes. Prepare 3 to 4 cups vegetables, selecting from these suggestions:

potatoes   carrots   onions   parsnips   turnips   rutabagas

Cut vegetables into uniform sizes; all should be about the size of a quartered onion. Place vegetables atop and around roast. Cover again and continue cooking. Allow to stand for 10 to 15 minutes, covered, after cooking time has elapsed. Carve and serve meat with vegetables and cooking liquid spooned over. Makes 2 to 3 servings per pound of meat.

ROAST BEEF
it browns beautifully to a juicy tenderness

Choose an evenly shaped boneless or bone-in roast weighing 2 to 8 pounds. Fat, if any, should be in a fairly even layer, trimmed to less than 1/2 inch thickness, if necessary. Boneless roasts require only a single turn. Roasts containing a large bone will require an extra turn to assure even cooking.

Some tender roasts that are good candidates for microwave cooking include the cross rib (boneless rolled roast from a tender portion of the chuck), rib eye or standing rib, sirloin tip and even good quality rump roasts. Less tender roasts should be cooked with moist heat, in the style of the chuck roast on page 19.

1 — Season the roast before cooking with freshly ground pepper, slivered or pressed garlic or crumbled herbs. *Salt after cooking,* as salt on the meat during cooking may cause the surface to be dry and tough.

2 — Calculate roasting time as follows:

      RARE — 4 to 6 minutes per pound (meat thermometer or probe registers 118 to 120° internal temperature), see note

      MEDIUM — 6 to 8 minutes per pound (130 to 140° internal temperature)

      WELL DONE — 8 to 10 minutes per pound (150 to 155° internal temperature)

3 — To roast, place meat, fat side down, on a microwave roasting rack in a shallow baking dish. Microwave, *uncovered,* at FULL POWER 5 minutes. Turn meat fat side up. Insert microwave thermometer or meat probe, parallel to oven bottom, 1 to 2 inches deep, depending on size of roast (thermometer should not reach exact center of a large roast, as this may give a misleading reading). Continue cooking, *uncovered,* at 3/4 POWER to desired doneness (times in chart include first 5 minutes).

If your microwave oven does not have variable power, microwave at FULL POWER, using lesser time in chart. Turn roast a second time during last half of cooking.

4 — Allow a standing time of 10 to 15 minutes after the roast is cooked. Keep it warm with a loose covering of foil to hold the heat in. During standing, the internal temperature will usually increase as much as 10°. Salt before carving. Makes 2 to 3 servings per pound of meat.

Note: Do not use a conventional mercury roast meat thermometer in a microwave oven. Look for microwave-safe "bi-therm" thermometers such as those made by Taylor and Cooper. These are designed to be used especially for microwave cooking, and most microwave oven manufacturers make them available as an accessory. Some microwave ovens have an automatic meat thermometer or probe. Insert the probe parallel to the oven bottom. Instead of calculating minutes per pound, the probe can be set for desired internal meat temperature. When it is reached, the oven automatically shuts off.

FAVORITE FAMILY MEAT LOAF
bake in a ring mold and serve with garden fresh peas in the center

1 pound ground lean beef
1 slice bread, crumbled
1/2 green pepper, seeded and chopped
1 medium onion, chopped
1 clove garlic, minced or pressed
1/2 cup finely chopped parsley
2 eggs, beaten
1/2 cup tomato sauce (or substitute catsup, if you wish)
1/4 teaspoon *each* salt and pepper
1/4 cup catsup
1 tablespoon *each* prepared mustard and brown sugar

Lightly mix ground beef, bread, green pepper, onion, garlic, parsley, beaten eggs, tomato sauce, salt and pepper. Loosely pack mixture into glass or ceramic loaf dish. Mix catsup, mustard and brown sugar; pour evenly over meat loaf. Microwave, *uncovered,* at FULL POWER 8 to 10 minutes. Allow to stand 5 to 8 minutes before slicing. Makes 5 to 6 servings.

Note: A meat loaf cooks even better in a ring mold. If you wish, place a glass custard cup in the center of a round pie or cake dish. Eliminating the center helps to cook the meat loaf evenly throughout.

CHILES RELLENOS CASSEROLE
this recipe features an easy way to cook hamburger

1 pound ground beef
1 small onion, chopped
2 cans (4 oz. *each*) whole green chiles
1-1/2 cups shredded Cheddar cheese
4 eggs
1 cup half-and-half (light cream)
1/2 cup water
1 teaspoon salt
Dash pepper
1/8 teaspoon Tabasco sauce

Crumble beef into a plastic colander; mix in onion. Place colander in a large bowl. Microwave, *uncovered,* at FULL POWER 4 to 5 minutes, stirring if necessary, until pink color is gone from meat; discard fat collected in bowl. Drain green chiles. Cut in halves lengthwise; remove seeds. Place half of the chiles in a 10- by 6-inch baking dish. Sprinkle with cheese. Cover with meat mixture. Arrange remaining chiles over meat.

Beat eggs; mix in half-and-half, water, salt, pepper and Tabasco sauce. Pour egg mixture over chiles. Microwave, *uncovered,* at FULL POWER 10 to 11 minutes, until center is almost set. Allow to stand 5 to 8 minutes before serving. Makes 6 servings.

STIR-FRY BEEF
serve with rice or spoon into pita bread for a hot sandwich

1 pound beef steak, such as top round, top sirloin or flank steak
1/4 cup soy sauce
2 cloves garlic, minced or pressed
1-inch piece fresh ginger root, peeled and thinly sliced
1 medium onion, slivered
1 green pepper, seeded and cut into strips
1/2 pound bean sprouts, rinsed and well drained
3/4 cup regular-strength beef broth
1 tablespoon cornstarch
Dash Tabasco sauce
1/4 teaspoon freshly ground pepper
1/8 teaspoon salt
1 tablespoon salad oil

Slice the beef, cutting on the diagonal, into very thin strips, about 1/16th inch thick (freeze meat partially for ease in cutting thin slices). Marinate beef strips in mixture of soy sauce, garlic and ginger for at least 1 hour.

In 2-quart casserole combine onion, green pepper and bean sprouts. Microwave, *covered,* at FULL POWER 2 minutes; set aside. In 1-cup measure combine beef broth, cornstarch, Tabasco, pepper and salt; mix well with a wire whisk. Microwave, *uncovered,* at FULL POWER 2 minutes; whisk until smooth and set aside.

Preheat microwave browning dish (see page 12) in microwave oven at FULL POWER 4 minutes. Add oil. Quickly stir in marinated beef mixture; stir well. Microwave, *uncovered,* at FULL POWER 2 minutes. Stir again; meat should be browned and just cooked. Mix in cooked vegetables and prepared sauce; stir to blend. If necessary, reheat, *uncovered,* in microwave oven at FULL POWER 1 to 2 minutes. Makes 3 to 4 servings.

PIZZA FONDUE

so easy even children can prepare it

1 pound ground chuck
1 small onion, chopped
1/2 teaspoon garlic salt
2 cans (10 oz. *each*) pizza sauce
1-1/2 cups shredded natural Cheddar cheese
1 cup shredded natural mozzarella cheese
Cubed French bread

Crumble ground beef into a plastic colander; mix in onion. Place colander in a large bowl. Microwave, *uncovered,* at **FULL POWER** 4 to 5 minutes, until pink color is gone from meat; discard fat collected in bowl. Transfer meat to casserole or ceramic fondue dish. Mix in remaining ingredients except bread. Microwave, *uncovered,* at **FULL POWER** 5 to 7 minutes, until cheeses melt and fondue bubbles. Stir to blend mixture. Serve with bread cubes to twirl in mixture. Return to microwave oven to reheat, if necessary, or place over burner to keep warm while serving. Makes 4 to 5 servings.

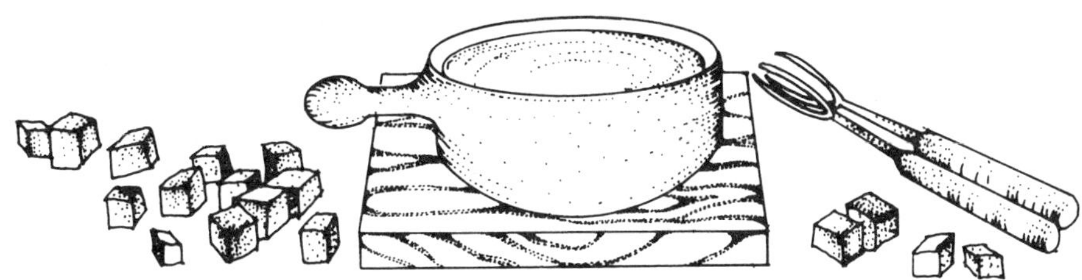

PORK CHOPS WITH BARBECUE SAUCE

you will be amazed at how juicy and tender pork chops can be

1 medium onion, sliced
2 cloves garlic, minced or pressed
1/2 cup catsup
2 tablespoons white or cider vinegar
1/2 teaspoon Worcestershire sauce
1/8 teaspoon *each* salt and pepper
6 loin pork chops, cut 1 inch thick

For the sauce, place onion and garlic in 1-quart casserole. Microwave, *covered*, at FULL POWER 1 to 2 minutes, until soft. Stir in catsup, vinegar, Worcestershire sauce, salt and pepper. Microwave, *uncovered*, at FULL POWER 3 minutes; stir and set sauce aside.

Arrange pork chops in shallow oblong baking dish just large enough to hold them in a single layer, placing meatier parts to the outside. Cover chops evenly with cooked sauce. Cover dish loosely with a piece of waxed paper. Microwave at FULL POWER 12 to 14 minutes, rotating dish as necessary; *or* microwave at 3/4 POWER 14 to 18 minutes. Allow to stand 5 minutes before serving. Makes 6 servings.

LARAINE'S FRUIT-STUFFED GLAZED HAM
a slice of this ham reveals fruits baked in the center

5-pound canned ham
1 package (8 to 10 oz.) mixed dried fruits
1/2 cup golden raisins
1 small can (8-1/4 oz.) chunk pineapple, drained
3/4 cup chopped pecans or walnuts
2 tablespoons *each* brown sugar, frozen orange juice concentrate (thawed) and sherry
1/4 teaspoon ground cloves

Drain ham and slice it in half horizontally, sandwich style. Finely chop the mixed dried fruits; mix them with raisins, pineapple and nuts. Spread the fruit mixture over the cut side of the bottom piece of ham. Cover with top half, sandwich-fashion. Secure in place with several long bamboo skewers. Place in shallow baking dish. Mix together brown sugar, orange juice concentrate, sherry and cloves. Spoon half the sugar mixture over ham.

Microwave, *uncovered,* at FULL POWER 10 minutes. Reduce to HALF POWER and continue cooking 17 to 20 minutes more. (If cooking at FULL POWER for entire cooking period, give baking dish a half turn several times. Reduce total cooking time to 15 to 20 minutes.) Drizzle with remaining sugar mixture throughout cooking time until it is used. Let stand 5 to 10 minutes before carving. Slice about 3/4 inch thick to serve. Makes 10 to 12 servings.

SAUSAGE FONDUE
tortilla chips replace the traditional French bread

1 pound bulk pork sausage
2 tablespoons flour
1 pound natural Monterey jack cheese, shredded (about 4 cups)
1 pound natural Cheddar cheese, shredded (about 4 cups)
3/4 cup dry white wine
2 teaspoons chili powder
Tortilla chips or corn chips

Crumble sausage into a plastic colander. Place colander in a large bowl. Microwave, *uncovered*, at FULL POWER 6 to 7 minutes, until pink color is completely gone from meat; discard fat collected in bowl and transfer sausage to large casserole. Stir in flour and cheeses. Microwave, *uncovered*, 2 to 3 minutes. Blend in wine and chili powder; cook 6 to 7 minutes more, stirring occasionally, until cheese melts and fondue bubbles. Serve with tortilla or corn chips to scoop up fondue. Return to microwave oven to reheat, if necessary, or place in fondue pan over burner to keep warm while serving. Makes 4 to 5 servings.

ROAST GLAZED LEG OF LAMB
serve this Greek-accented lamb accompanied by Pilaf with Mushrooms, page 49

3 cloves garlic
1 leg of lamb, 5 to 7 pounds
Freshly ground pepper
1 teaspoon crumbled oregano

1/3 cup lemon juice
1 teaspoon soy sauce
Chopped parsley, for garnish

Cut 1 clove of garlic in half and rub cut sides over all surfaces of lamb. Sprinkle meat with pepper and oregano. Mince or press remaining 2 cloves garlic and mix with lemon juice and soy sauce. Place lamb, fat side down, on a microwave roasting rack in a shallow baking dish.

Microwave, *uncovered,* at FULL POWER 8 minutes. Turn roast, fat side up. Pour half of the lemon juice mixture over roast. Insert microwave thermometer or meat probe, if used, parallel to oven bottom in center of the thickest part of the roast. Continue cooking, *uncovered,* at 3/4 POWER to desired doneness (times in chart include first 8 minutes) as follows, *or* at FULL POWER 5 to 6 minutes per pound.

RARE — 7 minutes per pound (meat thermometer or probe registers 140° internal temperature), see note, page 21.

MEDIUM — 9 minutes per pound (160° internal temperature)

Drizzle with remaining lemon juice mixture several times during last half of cooking time. Allow roast to stand, loosely covered with foil, 10 to 15 minutes before carving. During standing, the internal temperature will usually increase as much as 10°. Sprinkle with parsley, carve and serve with skimmed cooking liquid in a sauceboat to spoon over sliced meat. Makes 6 to 8 servings.

LEMON-BUTTER CHICKEN BREASTS
serve with a salad of fresh summer fruits

2 whole chicken breasts, cut into halves (about 2 lbs. total)
Paprika and pepper
1 lemon
Salt
2 tablespoons butter or margarine
1 clove garlic, minced or pressed
2 tablespoons chopped parsley

Remove skin from chicken pieces; bone, if desired. Sprinkle chicken with paprika and pepper (do not salt at this time). Place chicken on microwave roasting rack in shallow baking dish, arranging meatier portions to outside edges of dish and placing pieces about 1 inch apart. Cut lemon in half and squeeze juice over chicken breasts. Microwave, *uncovered,* at FULL POWER 9 to 11 minutes, until chicken tests done. Remove from microwave oven and allow to stand 3 to 4 minutes. Sprinkle lightly with salt.

Meanwhile, place butter, garlic and parsley in glass measuring cup. Microwave, *uncovered,* at FULL POWER 1 to 2 minutes, until butter melts and garlic is soft. Pour butter sauce over chicken. Makes 4 servings.

CHICKEN BAKED IN TOMATO SAUCE
accompany this mildly spicy dish with a green salad

1 frying chicken (about 3 lbs.), cut up
Paprika
2 tablespoons olive oil
1/2 pound mushrooms, sliced
1 green pepper, seeded and chopped
1 clove garlic, minced or pressed
1 medium onion, chopped
2 stalks celery, chopped
1 can (1 lb.) tomatoes
6 drops Tabasco sauce
1 tablespoon Worcestershire sauce
1 can (6 oz.) tomato paste
Cooked rice

Remove skin from chicken pieces. Arrange chicken on a microwave roasting rack in a shallow baking dish with meatier pieces toward the outside. Sprinkle with paprika. Cover loosely with waxed paper. Microwave at FULL POWER 8 minutes. Rearrange chicken, placing less cooked pieces toward outside edge of rack. Cover again with waxed paper. Microwave at FULL POWER 6 to 8 minutes longer, until chicken tests done; set aside.

Mix together olive oil, mushrooms, green pepper, garlic, onion and celery in a 2-quart casserole or measuring cup. Microwave, *uncovered,* at FULL POWER 3 minutes; stir. Mix in tomatoes, Tabasco sauce, Worcestershire sauce and tomato paste. Microwave, *uncovered,* at FULL POWER 6 minutes; stir well.

Transfer chicken pieces to an oblong baking dish. Pour on tomato sauce. Microwave, *uncovered,* at FULL POWER 3 to 4 minutes, until very hot throughout. Serve with rice. Makes 4 to 5 servings.

ROAST TURKEY
now you can enjoy turkey *anytime*

Imagine cooking a 12-pound turkey in about 1 hour and 45 minutes! With a microwave oven this amazing sounding feat is no trick at all, and the turkey will be moister and juicier than you have ever believed possible.

Choose a turkey weighing less than 15 pounds for ease in handling. This is also a size that fits easily into most microwave ovens. The turkey may be cooked with or without stuffing; the overall cooking time will be the same.

1 — Sprinkle salt and pepper inside breast and body cavities of a 9- to 15-pound turkey (for tips on thawing frozen turkey, see page 9). Do not salt outside, as this may dry and toughen the skin. Sprinkle skin lightly with paprika.

2 — If you wish, fill breast and body cavities with your favorite stuffing. Hold stuffing in place with the crust end of a loaf of bread (discard it before serving).

3 — Place prepared turkey, breast down, in large baking dish. (It is not necessary to use a roasting rack.) Have ready a bulb baster to remove cooking juices as they accumulate in baking dish (save juices for gravy or to use as broth in other dishes).

4 — Calculate roasting time from this formula: 9 minutes per pound at 3/4 **POWER** or 7 to 8 minutes per pound at **FULL POWER**. Divide total cooking time by 4.

5 — Microwave turkey, breast down, for 1/4 of the total estimated cooking time. Then turn turkey to balance it on one wing, with the other wing up (you may need to prop it to keep it in place; use glass measuring cups or coffee mugs). Now microwave it in this position for another 1/4 of the total estimated time. Remove and reserve juices that accumulate in the roasting dish from time to time; this will speed cooking and prevent messy spattering. Turn turkey to other side, with the other wing up; microwave for another 1/4 of the total estimated time.

6 — Finally, for the last 1/4 of the cooking time, turn the turkey with the breast up.

7 — Cover turkey lightly with foil and allow it to stand 15 to 20 minutes before carving.

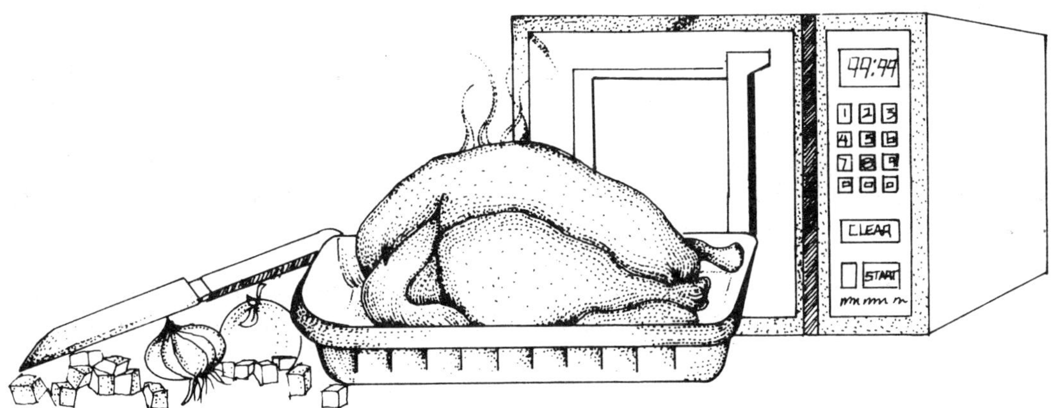

FESTIVE CORNISH HENS
an elegant way to cook 1 to 4 hens at a time

18- to 24-ounce frozen Rock Cornish game hens, thawed (page 9)
Salt and pepper
Orange marmalade
Sherry

Rinse Cornish hens and pat them dry. Sprinkle salt and pepper inside cavities. For glaze, mix marmalade and sherry, using about 1 teaspoon sherry and 1 tablespoon marmalade per hen. Place Cornish hens, breasts up, on a microwave roasting rack in a shallow baking dish, allowing about 1 inch of space between hens if cooking more than one. Brush with about half of the glaze.

Microwave, *uncovered,* at FULL POWER 10 to 15 minutes per hen, turning baking dish as needed for even cooking. Interrupt cooking several times to brush with additional glaze. Cornish hens are done when drumsticks move easily, and juices run clear from thickest part when tested with point of a small sharp knife. Cover lightly with foil and allow to stand 5 to 10 minutes before serving.

BUTTERFISH WITH CHEESE AND TOMATO SAUCE

only a microwave oven can cook butterfish to such firm, moist perfection

1 pound butterfish fillets (about 2 large fillets), see note
1 tablespoon finely chopped onion
1/2 teaspoon salt
1/8 teaspoon pepper
1 medium tomato, peeled, seeded and finely chopped
1/2 cup shredded Swiss cheese
1 tablespoon butter or margarine, melted

If fish fillets are large, cut into serving-sized pieces. Arrange fish in shallow baking dish or casserole with larger pieces at outer edges and smaller pieces in center. Sprinkle with onion, salt and pepper. Top with tomato and cheese; drizzle butter over all. Microwave, *loosely covered*, at FULL POWER 7 to 9 minutes, until fish is still firm but flakes easily when tested with a fork. Do not overcook or fish becomes too soft. Makes 4 to 5 servings.

Note: If butterfish is not available, you can substitute ocean perch, sole or red snapper fillets.

TUNA PILAF
a one-dish meal the family will love

1 medium onion, thinly sliced
2 stalks celery, thinly sliced diagonally
1 tablespoon butter or margarine
1 package (10 oz.) frozen mixed vegetables
3 cups cooked rice (see note)
2 cans (6-1/2 oz. *each*) chunk light tuna, drained
1 can (5 oz.) water chestnuts, drained and sliced
1/4 cup soy sauce

Place onion, celery and butter in 2-quart casserole. Microwave, *covered,* at FULL POWER 2 minutes. Add frozen vegetables. Cover again and microwave at FULL POWER 5 minutes; stir. Mix in rice, tuna, water chestnuts and soy sauce. Microwave, *loosely covered,* at FULL POWER 6 to 8 minutes, until steaming hot. Makes 6 to 8 servings.

Note: Cooking rice in a microwave oven is not a time saver, but it is convenient. Cleanup is easy, too, as the rice will not stick to the cooking container.

For 3 cups cooked rice, place 1 cup rice and 2 cups water in a large casserole (3-quart size or larger). Microwave, *covered,* at FULL POWER 13 to 15 minutes. Allow to stand 5 minutes to absorb all the liquid. Stir; season to taste with salt and butter or margarine.

ITALIAN SHRIMP SAUTÉ

marvelous with rice and a crisp green vegetable

1/4 cup butter or margarine
1 clove garlic, minced or pressed
2 tablespoons lemon juice
1 pound large shrimp or prawns, peeled and deveined
1/4 teaspoon salt
1/8 teaspoon pepper
2 tablespoons chopped parsley

Put butter, garlic and lemon juice in a medium-sized casserole or baking dish. Microwave, *uncovered*, at **FULL POWER** 45 seconds, until butter melts. Lightly mix in shrimp. Microwave, *uncovered*, at **FULL POWER** 2 to 3 minutes. Stir gently; shrimp should be pink and tender. If necessary, return to microwave oven and cook as much as 1 minute longer. Mix in salt, pepper and parsley. Makes about 3 servings.

Egg and Cheese Dishes

POACHED EGGS
a quick beginning for a Sunday breakfast

1 cup water
4 eggs
Buttered toast
Salt and pepper

Measure 1/4 cup water into each of 4 individual custard cups or coffee mugs. Microwave, *uncovered*, at FULL POWER 1-1/2 minutes, until water is very hot. Break 1 egg into center of each container of hot water. Pierce each egg yolk with a fork to allow steam to escape (the yolk will not run).

Cover cooking containers with small pieces of waxed paper. Microwave at FULL POWER 1-1/2 to 2 minutes, or to preferred doneness. Always undercook eggs slightly as they will continue to cook before you can eat them! Serve on toast and season with salt and pepper. Makes 4 servings.

BAKED EGGS IN MUSHROOM SAUCE
these cheese-topped eggs make a perfect brunch or luncheon dish

1/4 pound mushrooms, sliced
2 tablespoons butter or margarine
2 to 3 green onions, sliced (use green tops)
2 tablespoons flour
1/2 cup milk
1/8 teaspoon crumbled marjoram

1/2 teaspoon liquid brown-gravy seasoning
1/4 teaspoon salt
1/8 teaspoon pepper
4 eggs
1/4 cup grated Parmesan cheese

Place sliced mushrooms, butter and green onions in a mixing bowl or large measuring cup. Microwave, *uncovered,* at FULL POWER 3 minutes. Stir in flour, milk, marjoram, gravy seasoning, salt and pepper; mix to blend. Microwave at FULL POWER 3 to 4 minutes, until thickened; mix well with a wire whisk.

Divide sauce evenly into 4 small au gratin dishes or other shallow individual casseroles. Break 1 egg into the center of each. Pierce each egg yolk gently with a fork to allow steam to escape (the yolk will not run). Sprinkle with cheese. Microwave, *uncovered,* at 3/4 POWER 3 to 4 minutes, *or* at FULL POWER 2 to 3 minutes, until eggs are just set. Allow to stand 2 to 3 minutes. Makes 4 servings.

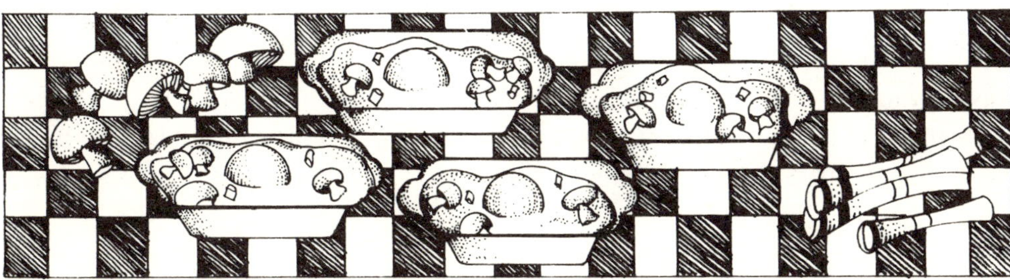

EGGS FLORENTINE
spinach has never looked or tasted better

1 bunch fresh spinach (about 1-1/4 lbs.), *or*
   1 package (10 oz.) frozen chopped spinach
2 tablespoons *each* butter or margarine and flour
2 cups milk

1/4 teaspoon *each* salt and pepper
6 eggs
1/4 cup grated Parmesan cheese
Chopped parsley, for garnish

Rinse fresh spinach and tear into bite-sized pieces. Place in covered 1-quart casserole. Microwave, *covered,* at FULL POWER 3 minutes; set aside. To cook frozen spinach, place frozen block in casserole and microwave, *covered,* at FULL POWER 4 to 5 minutes, until just barely cooked; stir and set aside.

For the white sauce, place butter and flour in 4-cup (or larger) measuring cup or bowl. Microwave, *uncovered,* at FULL POWER 30 to 45 seconds. Mix well with a wire whisk, then stir in milk, salt and pepper. Microwave at FULL POWER 3 to 4 minutes; whisk well. This should have the consistency of a medium white sauce.

Drain and discard any liquid from the spinach. Add 1/2 cup of the sauce to the spinach; mix well. Divide spinach mixture evenly into 6 custard cups or individual casseroles. Break 1 egg into the center of each. Pierce each egg yolk gently with a fork to allow steam to escape (the yolk will not run). Cover evenly with remaining white sauce; sprinkle with grated cheese. Arrange dishes in a circle in microwave oven. Cover loosely with waxed paper. Microwave at 3/4 POWER 4 to 6 minutes, *or* 2 to 3 minutes at FULL POWER, until eggs are cooked to your liking. Sprinkle with parsley and serve. Makes 6 servings.

QUICK COMPANY QUICHE
a leek-filled pie to delight your guests

1 package (8 oz.) refrigerator crescent rolls
1 bunch (4 to 5) leeks
4 eggs
1 cup milk or half-and-half (light cream)
1-1/2 cups shredded Swiss cheese
1/4 teaspoon salt
1/8 teaspoon white pepper

Unroll crescent rolls and arrange them to form a complete crust on bottom and sides of 9- to 11-inch glass or ceramic quiche dish or 9-inch pie plate. Pinch the seams together to seal.

Cut leeks into 1/4-inch slices, using tender light green portion of the tops but discarding tougher top parts. Place leeks in small casserole or bowl; cover with lid or loosely with waxed paper. Microwave at **FULL POWER** 3 to 4 minutes, until leeks are tender; drain, discarding liquid. In a bowl beat eggs well; mix in cooked leeks and remaining ingredients. Pour into unbaked shell. Microwave, *uncovered*, at **FULL POWER** 8 to 9 minutes, rotating dish 2 or 3 times if necessary to cook evenly; *or* cook at 3/4 **POWER** 10 to 11 minutes. Allow to stand 5 to 8 minutes, then cut into wedges to serve. Makes 6 main-dish servings.

MEXICAN QUICHE
the chile powder gives the crust a festive look

9-inch baked pastry shell (recipe follows)
3 eggs
1 cup milk or half-and-half (light cream)
1/4 teaspoon salt
1/8 teaspoon ground cumin
1 small can (4 oz.) chopped green chiles
2 cups shredded Monterey jack cheese
1 cup shredded Cheddar cheese

Prepare pastry shell. Beat eggs. Mix in remaining ingredients, reserving 1/4 cup of the Cheddar cheese for the top. Pour mixture into baked pastry shell. Sprinkle with reserved Cheddar cheese. Microwave, *uncovered,* at FULL POWER 9 to 12 minutes, until filling is almost set. Allow to stand 8 to 10 minutes, then cut into wedges to serve. Makes 6 servings.

Baked Pastry Shell: In a bowl mix 1 cup unsifted all-purpose flour and 1/2 teaspoon *each* salt and chile powder. Cut in 6 tablespoons butter or margarine until mixture has the consistency of coarse crumbs. Gradually stir in 1/4 cup cold water until dough begins to cling together. Form dough into a ball. Roll out into a 10-inch circle on a lightly floured board or pastry cloth. Carefully transfer to an 8-inch quiche dish or pie plate, being careful not to stretch pastry. Trim and flute edge. Pierce sides and bottom of pastry all over with fork tines. Microwave, *uncovered,* at 3/4 POWER 8 to 10 minutes, *or* at FULL POWER 6 to 8 minutes, until pastry looks dry. It will not brown, but will be flaky and crisp when cool.

CHEESE FONDUE
delicious and foolproof—it doesn't scorch or separate and reheats beautifully!

4 cups shredded natural Swiss or Gruyère cheese
1-1/2 tablespoons flour
1/4 teaspoon *each* nutmeg and white pepper
2 cups dry white wine
2 tablespoons Kirsch (clear cherry brandy)
Cubed French bread

Mix together cheese, flour, nutmeg and pepper in a 1-quart bowl or ceramic fondue dish. Microwave, *uncovered,* at FULL POWER 6 to 8 minutes, until cheese is melted. Stir well. Gradually mix in wine and Kirsch. Reheat at FULL POWER 2 to 3 minutes until fondue bubbles gently. Serve immediately with cubed French bread to twirl in mixture. Return to microwave oven to reheat, if necessary, or place fondue dish over warmer while serving. Makes about 4 servings.

Vegetables - More Delicious than Ever

Most fresh vegetables except beans can be cooked, covered, without additional water. However when cooking fresh green beans and lima beans, add 1 to 2 tablespoons water.

Do not salt vegetables until cooking is finished. You will discover very little salt is needed because microwaved vegetables retail their full natural flavor.

When preparing vegetables, cut them into even sizes and shapes. Arrange any smaller pieces in the center and larger pieces to the outside in the cooking vessel. Place the tougher parts, such as broccoli stems, toward the outside edge, with the tender tips toward the center.

A combination of vegetables can be cooked in the same dish, as long as they are cut into equal sizes and shapes.

Once you cook vegetables in your microwave oven you'll never want to cook them any other way. Vegetables prepared this way retain their colors, cook to a crisp tenderness and are truly more delicious than ever! Here is just a sampling.

ARTICHOKES
serve with clarified butter for dipping

Cut off stems and tops; trim prickly leaf tips. Rinse thoroughly. Place prepared artichokes, tops down, into deep bowl or casserole in a single layer. Microwave, *covered,* at FULL POWER, allowing 5 minutes per medium artichoke. When done, a fork should penetrate the heart easily; if it resists, continue cooking 1 minute longer. (Leave any dark, small or bruised outer leaves on during cooking; remove them just before serving.) Four artichokes will take about 12 to 14 minutes.

ASPARAGUS
green, green, green

Thoroughly rinse and trim woody ends of asparagus spears. Arrange in shallow baking dish with larger parts toward outer edge. Microwave, *covered,* at FULL POWER, allowing 4 to 5 minutes per pound. Season to taste with butter, salt and pepper.

CARROTS
naturally sweet and rich in vitamin A

Rinse and scrape carrots; slice evenly about 1/2 inch thick. Place in casserole. Microwave, *covered,* at FULL POWER, allowing 1-1/2 minutes per carrot. Season to taste.

CAULIFLOWER
delicious drenched with hollandaise or mornay sauce

To cook whole: Rinse and remove leaves from a 1-1/2-pound cauliflower. Use a sharp knife to cut out core. Place upside-down in pie plate or rimmed dish. Microwave, *covered,* at FULL POWER 9 to 11 minutes. Allow to stand 2 to 3 minutes. Season to taste.

To cook cut up: Remove leaves and core. Cut into bite-sized pieces. Place in casserole or serving dish. Microwave, *covered,* at FULL POWER 6 to 7 minutes. Season to taste.

CORN-ON-THE-COB
choose one of three methods—all taste deliciously fresh

To cook in husks: Carefully peel back husks halfway; remove silk. Rinse. Replace some of the husks to cover kernels. Place ears in microwave oven in a single layer. Microwave at FULL POWER, allowing 3 minutes per ear. Allow to stand 1 to 2 minutes; serve with butter and other seasonings to taste. Four medium ears will take 9 to 10 minutes.

To cook in paper or plastic wrap: Remove and discard husks and silk; rinse. Wrap corn gently with waxed paper or plastic wrap. Microwave at FULL POWER, allowing 3 minutes per ear as above.

To cook in a covered dish: Remove and discard husks and silk; rinse. Place corn in a large casserole. Microwave, *covered,* at FULL POWER, allowing 3 minutes per ear as above.

PARSLIED POTATOES
serve with Steak with Fresh Mushrooms, page 18

4 medium white potatoes (preferably white rose variety)
Salt and pepper
Butter or margarine
Chopped parsley, for garnish

Peel potatoes and cut into uniform chunks (or, if you wish, scrub and cook unpeeled). Place in 2-quart casserole or large measuring cup. Microwave, *covered,* at FULL POWER 9 to 11 minutes, until potatoes are fork tender. Season to taste with salt, pepper and butter and sprinkle with parsley. Makes 4 servings.

BAKED POTATOES
ready in just minutes

Scrub baking potatoes. Pierce each potato in several places with a fork. Microwave, *uncovered,* at FULL POWER, allowing 4 minutes per medium-sized potato. Placing potatoes on a microwave roasting rack will enable them to cook more evenly and permit excess moisture to escape from under them. Four medium potatoes will take about 12 to 14 minutes.

BUTTERY MUSHROOMS
a welcome substitute for canned mushrooms

1/2 pound fresh mushrooms
1 tablespoon butter or margarine
Salt and pepper

Rinse mushrooms and pat dry; slice. Place mushrooms and butter in a 1-quart casserole. Microwave, *covered,* at FULL POWER 2 to 3 minutes, until butter melts and mushrooms are tender. Season with salt and pepper to taste. Serve as a side dish or as a mushroom sauce for steak and other meats and poultry, or mix with cooked vegetables. Makes about 1 cup.

Note: In recipes calling for a can of mushrooms, substitute this recipe for economy and better flavor.

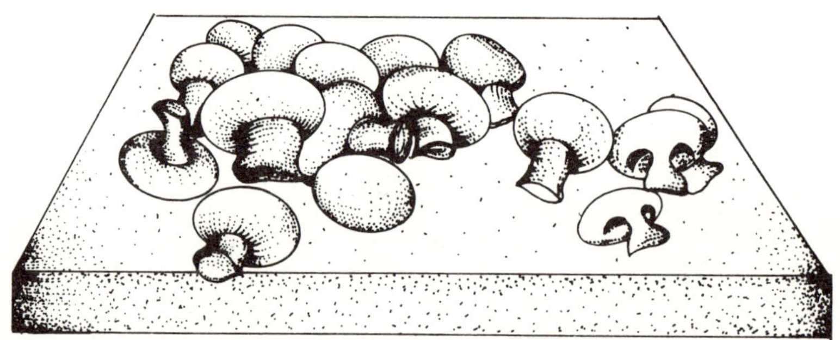

PILAF WITH MUSHROOMS
make early in the day and reheat for dinner in just 5 to 6 minutes

1 medium onion, finely chopped
2 cloves garlic, minced or pressed
1/2 cup (1/4 lb.) butter or margarine
3 tablespoons finely chopped parsley
1/4 teaspoon *each* crumbled marjoram and thyme
1 cup long-grain white rice
1-1/2 cups regular-strength chicken or beef broth
1/2 cup dry white wine
1 pound mushrooms, sliced
2 tablespoons lemon juice
1/2 cup grated Parmesan cheese

In a 3-quart casserole combine onion, garlic and butter. Microwave, *uncovered*, at FULL POWER 2 minutes. Mix in parsley, marjoram, thyme, rice, broth and wine. Microwave, *covered*, at FULL POWER 14 to 15 minutes. Allow to stand 8 to 10 minutes.

Meanwhile, mix together mushrooms and lemon juice in a 1-quart bowl or casserole. Microwave, *covered*, at FULL POWER 3 to 4 minutes. Add mushroom mixture to rice at the end of its standing period, fluff and serve sprinkled with cheese. Makes 5 to 6 servings.

ITALIAN EGGPLANT CASSEROLE
the eggplant is so flavorful and tender when cooked the microwave way

1 medium eggplant
1/4 cup butter or margarine
1 tablespoon flour
1 can (8 oz.) tomato sauce
1/4 teaspoon *each* salt, crumbled oregano and basil
1 clove garlic, minced or pressed
1/8 teaspoon pepper
1 cup sliced green onions (include green tops)
1/2 cup sliced ripe olives
2 cups shredded mozzarella cheese

Cut unpeeled eggplant into 1/2-inch cubes; set aside. Place butter in a large casserole (such as a 10-inch quiche dish or 2-quart oblong or rectangular baking dish) and microwave, *uncovered*, at FULL POWER 30 seconds. Add eggplant and mix to coat with butter; sprinkle with flour and mix to blend. Cover loosely with waxed paper. Microwave at FULL POWER 4 minutes.

Combine tomato sauce, salt, oregano, basil, garlic, pepper, green onions and 1/3 cup of the olives. Stir into eggplant mixture. Mix in 1-1/2 cups of the cheese. Microwave, *uncovered*, at FULL POWER 8 to 10 minutes. Sprinkle with remaining 1/2 cup cheese and remaining olives. Allow to stand 3 to 4 minutes before serving. Makes 4 to 6 servings.

RATATOUILLE

use this French-inspired dish as a filling for mushroom caps

1 medium eggplant
1 clove garlic, minced or pressed
1 medium onion, chopped
1 green pepper, seeded and chopped
1/4 teaspoon crumbled basil
1/2 teaspoon salt

1/4 teaspoon pepper
2 tablespoons olive oil
1 can (8 oz.) tomato sauce
1/4 cup sliced ripe olives
1/2 cup freshly grated Parmesan cheese
Cooked rice

Cut off stem and blossom ends of eggplant. Place whole eggplant on a plate in microwave oven and microwave, *uncovered,* at FULL POWER 7 to 10 minutes, rotating once if necessary for even cooking; set aside until cool enough to handle.

In a 2-quart casserole or large measuring cup or serving bowl combine garlic, onion, green pepper, basil, salt, pepper and olive oil; microwave, *uncovered,* at FULL POWER 3 minutes. Mix in tomato sauce, olives and Parmesan cheese. Peel cooked eggplant and cut into 1-inch cubes; add to sauce mixture. Microwave, *uncovered,* at FULL POWER 2 to 3 minutes. Serve as a vegetable main dish with rice. Makes 4 to 6 servings.

Note: If you wish, cooked eggplant can also be mashed and stirred into sauce to serve as an appetizer with crackers. For Ratatouille Stuffed Mushrooms, fill mushroom caps with the mixture; for 6 to 8 mushrooms, microwave, *uncovered,* at FULL POWER 3 to 4 minutes.

SPINACH-NOODLE RING
your contribution to the next neighborhood potluck

1 package (10 oz.) frozen chopped spinach
1 package (12 oz.) medium noodles
1/2 cup (1/4 lb.) butter or margarine
1 cup sour cream
3 eggs, well beaten
Dash *each* salt and nutmeg

Defrost spinach in the package in microwave oven 2 to 3 minutes (see page 9), but do not cook; squeeze out excess moisture. Cook noodles conventionally according to package directions; drain well in a colander.

In a large bowl or casserole microwave butter, *uncovered*, at FULL POWER 30 seconds. Mix in thawed spinach, drained noodles and remaining ingredients. Pour mixture into a 6- to 8-cup ring mold or plastic bundt dish, brioche dish or other round dish (place a custard cup in center to make a ring, if necessary). Microwave, *uncovered*, at FULL POWER 10 to 13 minutes, *or* at 3/4 POWER 12 to 15 minutes, until set. Allow to stand 8 to 10 minutes before unmolding to serve. Makes 6 to 8 servings.

Desserts and Sweet Treats

CHERRIES JUBILEE
have the ice cream ready ahead of time, scooped into serving dishes

1 can (about 16 oz.) pitted dark sweet cherries
2 tablespoons sugar
Dash cinnamon
Juice and grated rind of 1 orange
1 tablespoon cornstarch
1/4 cup *each* Cognac or brandy and cherry-flavored brandy
Vanilla ice cream

Drain cherries, reserving 1 cup of the liquid (discard remainder). To the 1 cup cherry liquid in a 6- to 8-cup tempered glass mixing bowl or tempered glass serving bowl, add sugar, cinnamon, orange juice and rind and cornstarch; mix until smooth. Microwave, *uncovered,* at FULL POWER, until boiling, about 3 minutes. Lightly mix in cherries. Cook 1 minute longer, until cherries are heated through. Remove bowl from microwave oven.

In a tempered glass or ceramic measuring cup or individual casserole with a handle, combine Cognac and cherry brandy; heat slightly, *uncovered,* in a microwave oven at FULL POWER 30 seconds. Ignite and pour, flaming, over hot cherries. When flames have subsided, spoon cherry sauce over individual servings of ice cream. Makes 4 servings.

FRENCH CUSTARD

an elegant dessert, or a wonderful sauce for pound cake or fruit

2 eggs, separated
1/4 cup sugar
1 teaspoon cornstarch
1-1/2 cups milk
1/2 teaspoon vanilla
Floating Islands (recipe follows)

Reserving egg whites for Floating Islands, beat egg yolks, sugar and cornstarch well in a 2-quart bowl or large measuring cup. Using a wire whisk, gradually mix in milk. Microwave, *uncovered*, at FULL POWER 3 to 4 minutes, whisking after 3 minutes. Mixture should have the consistency of thick cream. Stir in vanilla. Pour into individual serving dishes and let cool. Serve topped with Floating Islands. Makes 3 to 4 servings.

Floating Islands: Beat reserved 2 egg whites until frothy. Gradually add 1/4 cup sugar and beat until fluffy peaks form. Drop by mounds onto a waxed paper-lined plate. Microwave, *uncovered*, at FULL POWER 1-1/2 minutes, until set when touched lightly. Slip cooked mounds onto cooled custard or other cooked, cooled puddings.

Note: Warm custard can also be served as a sauce for cakes or poached fruits. Makes about 2 cups.

PERSIMMON PUDDING WITH AMBER SAUCE
dessert fare for the holiday season

1 cup unsifted whole wheat or all-purpose flour
1 cup sugar
1 teaspoon cinnamon
2 teaspoons baking soda
1/4 teaspoon salt
1 cup chopped nuts (optional)
1 cup fully ripe mashed persimmon pulp

1/2 cup milk
3/4 teaspoon vanilla
1/4 teaspoon almond extract
1 tablespoon melted butter, margarine or
  shortening
Amber Sauce (recipe follows)

Mix together flour, sugar, cinnamon, baking soda and salt; add nuts and stir to coat with flour mixture. Blend in remaining ingredients except sauce. Pour into 6- to 8-cup ring mold, plastic bundt dish or brioche dish. Insert 3 or 4 long bamboo skewers into pudding, then place a piece of plastic wrap over the top and secure it to the sides of the dish to make a tent. Microwave at HALF POWER 15 minutes, *or* at FULL POWER 11 to 12 minutes, until top is set (some surface moistness may appear; this will be absorbed as the pudding cools). Allow to stand 20 to 30 minutes. Unmold and serve warm or at room temperature with Amber Sauce. Makes 10 to 12 servings.

Amber Sauce: In a 4-cup measuring cup or bowl, mix 1 cup brown sugar (firmly packed), 1/2 cup light corn syrup, 1/4 cup butter or margarine and 1/2 cup whipping cream. Microwave, *uncovered,* at FULL POWER 3 to 4 minutes. Stir well to blend; serve warm. Makes about 1-1/2 cups.

Note: If you wish, pudding can be refrigerated, then reheated to serve warm. Allow about 15 seconds per serving.

FRUIT PIES

select your favorite fruit for this easy-to-make pie

3 cups mashed or finely diced fresh or thawed
    frozen fruit, such as strawberries, raspberries,
    peaches, apricots, rhubarb or apples
Sugar: 1/2 to 1 cup, depending on sweetness
    of fruit
1 tablespoon lemon juice
3 tablespoons cornstarch (see note)
Crumb Crust (recipe follows)
Whipped cream or whipped topping

To fruit in a 1-1/2 to 2-quart bowl or large measuring cup, add sugar, lemon juice and cornstarch; mix thoroughly. Microwave, *uncovered*, at FULL POWER 7 to 9 minutes, until thickened, glossy and transparent. Stir lightly. Spread fruit mixture in prepared Crumb Crust. Refrigerate 2 to 3 hours. Serve garnished with whipped cream or topping. Makes 6 to 8 servings.

Crumb Crust: In a medium-sized bowl or casserole microwave 1/2 cup butter or margarine, *uncovered*, at FULL POWER 30 to 45 seconds, until it melts. Mix in 2 cups finely crushed graham cracker, vanilla wafer or chocolate wafer crumbs. Press crumb mixture firmly over bottom and sides of 9-inch pie plate, 9- to 11-inch quiche dish or other suitable pie dish. Microwave, *uncovered*, at FULL POWER 2-1/2 to 3 minutes; cool until firm before filling.

Note: Increase cornstarch to 4 tablespoons if fruit is very juicy.

CHOCOLATE FONDUE
what fun to dip fresh fruits and cake into chocolate

12 ounces milk chocolate or semisweet baking chocolate, coarsely chopped
3/4 cup whipping cream
3 tablespoons orange-flavored liqueur (such as
    Cointreau, Grand Marnier or Triple Sec),
    brandy or rum
2 medium bananas, peeled and sliced 3/4 inch thick
1-1/2 cups strawberries, cubed apples or seedless grapes
1-1/2 cups 1-inch cubes fresh pineapple (*or*, use
    canned pineapple chunks, packed in their own
    juice, well drained)
Pound cake, cut into 3/4-inch cubes

Place chocolate and cream in small glass or ceramic fondue dish or other tempered glass serving dish. Microwave, *uncovered*, at HALF POWER 2 to 3 minutes, until chocolate melts (if cooked at FULL POWER, interrupt cooking several times to stir well). Smoothly mix in orange-flavored liqueur, brandy or rum.

To serve, spear fruits or pound cake and dip into hot chocolate mixture with fondue forks or long bamboo skewers. Keep fondue hot over candle or other warmer; return to microwave oven to reheat, if necessary, while serving. Makes 6 to 8 servings.

RUSSIAN TEA CAKES
watch carefully—these cook quickly

1 cup (1/2 lb.) butter or margarine
1 egg
1 teaspoon vanilla
1/2 cup powdered sugar
2-1/2 cups unsifted all-purpose flour
1 cup finely chopped nuts
Powdered sugar

Place butter in a mixing bowl. Microwave, *uncovered,* at HALF POWER 30 seconds, until softened. (If your microwave oven does not have variable power, microwave at FULL POWER 15 seconds, rotate dish, and microwave 15 seconds longer at FULL POWER.) Beat well, add egg and mix until fluffy. Add vanilla and the 1/2 cup powdered sugar; beat well, until mixture is light and fluffy. Blend in flour and nuts; mix well. Shape dough into 1-inch balls. Arrange, 13 at a time, on a ceramic plate or glass pizza plate (place 10 cookies in outside ring with 3 in the center; avoid placing just 1 in the center).

Microwave, *uncovered,* at FULL POWER 2-1/2 to 3 minutes. Roll warm cookies in additional powdered sugar immediately, then cool. Roll again in sugar. Makes about 3 dozen.

BROWNIES
fudgy and good—loved by children and adults alike

1/2 cup (1/4 lb.) butter or margarine
2 squares (2 oz.) unsweetened chocolate
1 cup sugar
2 eggs
3/4 cup unsifted all-purpose flour
1/2 teaspoon *each* salt and vanilla
1/2 cup chopped nuts (optional, see note)

Place butter and chocolate in a medium-sized mixing bowl. Microwave, *uncovered*, at FULL POWER 1 minute, until melted. Add sugar and eggs; beat well. Blend in flour, salt, vanilla and nuts (if used). Spread batter in ungreased 8-inch-square baking dish or 2-quart oblong dish. Microwave, *uncovered*, at FULL POWER 7 minutes. Allow to stand 5 minutes. Cut into bars or squares. Makes 16 to 24 brownies.

Note: If nuts are omitted, decrease baking time to 6 minutes.

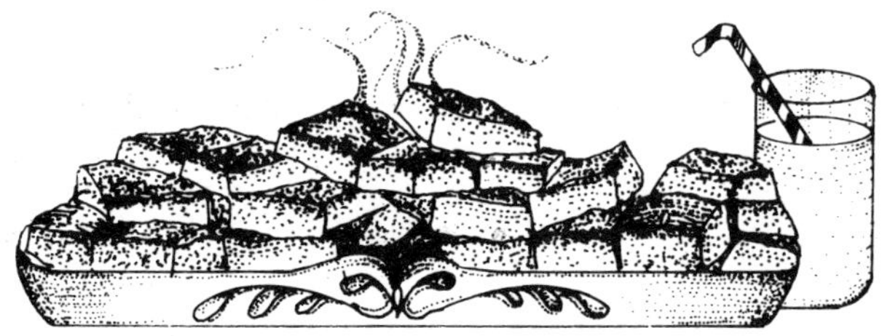

YOGURT CAKE WITH HONEY SAUCE
a honey glaze tops this moist, nutty cake

1 cup (1/2 lb.) butter
1-1/2 cups sugar
4 eggs
1 teaspoon grated lemon peel
1 teaspoon cinnamon
1 teaspoon vanilla
1 cup plain yogurt

2-1/2 cups unsifted all-purpose flour
1 teaspoon baking powder
1 teaspoon baking soda
1/4 teaspoon salt
1 cup chopped walnuts
Honey Sauce (recipe follows)

Place butter in a large mixing bowl. Microwave, *uncovered*, at HALF POWER 45 to 60 seconds, until softened. (If your microwave oven does not have variable power, microwave at FULL POWER 30 seconds, rotate dish, and microwave 30 seconds longer at FULL POWER.) Cream butter and sugar. Add all remaining ingredients and beat well. Pour into an ungreased ceramic or glass bundt dish or ring mold.

Microwave, *uncovered*, at 3/4 POWER 14 to 17 minutes, *or* at FULL POWER 10 to 13 minutes, rotating dish if necessary for even cooking. Allow to stand 10 minutes before inverting onto serving platter. Pierce top of cake with a fork in several places and pour sauce over. Makes 8 servings.

Honey Sauce: In a 2-cup measuring cup combine 1 cup sugar, 3/4 cup water and 1/4 cup honey. Microwave, *uncovered*, at FULL POWER 3 minutes. Stir in 3 tablespoons lemon juice or rum.

SPICED NUTS
this quick and delicious confection makes a memorable gift

3/4 cup brown sugar (firmly packed)
1 teaspoon cinnamon
1/2 teaspoon *each* salt and nutmeg
1/4 teaspoon *each* ground cloves and allspice
2 tablespoons water
1 cup *each* walnut and pecan halves and whole
   almonds (or any other combination making
   3 cups nuts)

In an 8-cup measure or other large tempered glass bowl mix sugar, spices, salt and water. Microwave, *uncovered,* at FULL POWER 3 minutes. Stir in nuts. Divide mixture in half. Return half of mixture to microwave oven at FULL POWER 3 to 4 minutes, stirring occasionally. Spread hot nut mixture in a single layer on a buttered plate to cool and crisp; break up with a fork. Repeat with second half. Makes about 3 cups.

TIMING GUIDE

Baby bottles, to warm	20 to 30 seconds at FULL POWER
Bacon	1 minute per slice at FULL POWER
	9 to 10 minutes per pound, cooked in layers, at FULL POWER
Brownies	5 to 7 minutes in 8-inch-square dish at FULL POWER (add 1 minute if recipe contains nuts)
Butter, clarified	45 to 60 seconds per 1/2 cup (1/4 lb.) at FULL POWER
Butter, melted	30 to 45 seconds per 1/2 cup (1/4 lb.) at FULL POWER
Butter, softened	15 seconds at FULL POWER, rotate dish, 15 more seconds at FULL POWER, or 30 seconds per 1/2 cup (1/4 lb.) at HALF POWER
Cakes, bundt	9 to 13 minutes at FULL POWER, or 14 to 17 minutes at 3/4 POWER, or 16 to 19 minutes at 3/4 POWER for heavy batters with fruits and nuts
Cakes, layer	4 to 6 minutes per layer at FULL POWER, or 5 to 7 minutes per layer at 3/4 POWER
Cakes, sheet	9 to 11 minutes (12- by 8-inch rectangular baking dish) at FULL POWER
Cakes, upside-down	7 to 9 minutes at FULL POWER
Casseroles, cooked ingredients	10 to 16 minutes for 2-quart casserole (about 2 minutes per cup) at FULL POWER
Chicken pieces	3 minutes per piece or 14 to 17 minutes for a 3- to 4-pound chicken, cut up, at FULL POWER
Chocolate, melted	1 to 1-1/2 minutes per 2 squares (2 oz.) at FULL POWER
Coconut, toasted	2 to 3 minutes at FULL POWER per cup
Cream cheese, softened	1 minute at HALF POWER per 3-ounce package
Crust, crumb	2 to 3 minutes per 9-inch crust at FULL POWER
Crust, pastry	5 to 7 minutes per 9-inch crust at FULL POWER, or 7 to 10 minutes at 3/4 POWER
Cupcakes	1 to 1-1/2 minutes per 6 to 7 cupcakes at FULL POWER
Eggs	1/2 to 3/4 minute per egg (*always* remove from shell to cook) at FULL POWER
Fish	about 4 minutes per pound at FULL POWER

Food	Time
Ham, canned	5 to 6 minutes per pound at FULL POWER, or 6 to 7 minutes per pound at 3/4 POWER
Ham, cured	7 to 8 minutes per pound at FULL POWER, or 12 to 13 minutes per pound at 3/4 POWER
Meat loaf	8 to 9 minutes per pound at FULL POWER 13 to 16 minutes for 2 pounds at FULL POWER
Milk, hot	1-1/2 to 2 minutes per cup at FULL POWER
Muffins	2 to 3 minutes per 6 to 7 muffins at FULL POWER
Nuts, toasted	2 to 3 minutes per 1/2 cup at FULL POWER
Onion, sautéed	2 to 3 minutes per medium onion, cooked in 1 tablespoon butter or margarine, at FULL POWER
Potatoes	3 to 5 minutes per potato at FULL POWER
Poultry, roast	7 to 9 minutes at FULL POWER per pound
Pudding	6 to 8 minutes per 4 servings at FULL POWER
Roasts, beef	4 to 6 minutes per pound at FULL POWER, or 4 to 9 minutes per pound, depending on desired doneness, at 3/4 POWER
Roasts, pork	7 to 8 minutes per pound at FULL POWER, or 10 to 13 minutes per pound at 3/4 POWER
Rolls, biscuits, doughnuts (to heat and freshen)	10 to 15 seconds per piece at FULL POWER
Sandwiches	20 to 30 seconds per sandwich at FULL POWER
Sauces	2 to 3 minutes per cup at FULL POWER
Seeds, toasted	2 to 3 minutes per cup, in 1/2 teaspoon butter or margarine, at FULL POWER
Soup	2 to 3 minutes per cup at FULL POWER
Syrup, to warm	15 to 30 seconds per cup at FULL POWER
Vegetables, canned	1 to 2 minutes per cup at FULL POWER
Vegetables, fresh	6 to 9 minutes per 4 servings at FULL POWER
Vegetables, frozen	4 to 8 minutes per 10-ounce package at FULL POWER
Water, boiling	2 to 4 minutes per cup at FULL POWER
Wieners	30 to 45 seconds per wiener at FULL POWER